KINGDOMS
OF THE
ORDINARY

1986

Agnes Lynch Starrett

Poetry Prize

KINGDOMS
of the
ORDINARY

Robley Wilson, Jr.

UNIVERSITY OF PITTSBURGH PRESS

Published by the University of Pittsburgh Press, Pittsburgh, Pa. 15260
Copyright © 1987, Robley Wilson, Jr.
All rights reserved
Feffer and Simons, Inc., London
Manufactured in the United States of America

Library of Congress Cataloging in Publication Data

Wilson, Robley.
  Kingdoms of the ordinary.

  (Pitt poetry series)
  I. Title. II. Series.
PS3573.I4665K5 1987   811'.54   87–5976
ISBN 0-8229-3557-0
ISBN 0-8229-5391-9 (pbk.)

8 1 1

wilson

Many of the poems in this collection first appeared, sometimes under different titles or in different form, in the following magazines: *The Atlantic* ("The Animals," "The Immortalist," and "The Rocking Chair"); *The Beloit Poetry Journal* ("The Emigré"); *The Carleton Miscellany* ("After Cards," "The Desire for Servants," "It Is Nothing to Live Alone," and "Mother Goose in a Late Age"); *Choice* ("I Know I Will Weep Forever"); *Dark Horse* ("Us and the Animals"); *Esquire* ("Armatures" and "October"); *The Georgia Review* ("Moving Back"); *The Iowa Review* ("The Military-Industrial Complex"); *Michigan Quarterly Review* ("Something of Love"); *The New Republic* ("A Woman"); *The North American Review* ("Bone," "Geode," "The Kingdom of the Ordinary," and "A Letter from Exile"); *The Ontario Review* ("Preserves"); *Open Places* ("The Persistence of Desire" and "The Wedding Ring"); *Perspective* ("A Fear of Children"); *Poetry* ("Endsong," "Hanging Curtains," "The Islands," "A Lady in Charcoal," "A Literary Lesson," "The Mozart Broadcast," "On Not Knowing the Names of the Flowers in Montana," "The Opera," "Recluse," "Sunday at the Shore," "The Suspense of Meeting," and "Three Dreams"); *Poetry Northwest* ("The Black Cat," "Demon Lovers," "The Marauder," and "Persons"); *Quest/79* ("Farm Pond"); *Raven* ("The Call of Some Creature"); *The Reporter* ("Weekends at the Cove"); *Shenandoah* ("Burning Over, Coming Back"). "At Night" first appeared in *Heartland II: Poets of the Midwest* (Northern Illinois University Press, 1975).

The author is indebted to Marvin Bell and to Chase Twichell, both of whom offered their encouragement and wisdom to the polishing and ordering of these poems.

The publication of this book is supported by grants from the National Endowment for the Arts in Washington, D.C., a Federal agency, and the Pennsylvania Council on the Arts.

CONTENTS

CONTENTS

KINGDOMS
OF THE
ORDINARY

THE REJOICING THAT ATTENDS THE MURDER OF FAMOUS MEN

The anonymous handsome
woman in the evening newsfilm
neither weeps nor bows.
Amid a general grief
she is some unbeliever
who looks out at us
past the shoulders of the stricken
and with tight lips and clear eyes
overbears us. She is ageless.
She has come among the first
to stand witness to tragedy,
the first whose mission it is
to teach us the rejoicing.

We find her offensive.
In the rainbows of our own
restricted visions, we curse
her detachment. If
we could put out our hands
and bridge the distance
between our chaos and her repose,
we would throttle her
and make her eyes bulge tears
like our own. If no one
stopped us, we would learn
the power sorrow confers
into the empty hands
we presently clench in our laps.

We see in this woman
the perverseness of history
and the unshatterable, solemn
dispassion of time—as if
indifference to evil were
the secret of immortality. She
is an insult to the mind,
cannot be got back at,
will not even tell her name.
If only she would go home
and in the privacy of her rooms
break down utterly!
But what we expect of history
we expect of her.

She is truly unshakeable;
in her heart's arrogance
she is glad for portentous death.
The anonymous handsome woman
in the newsfilms
is one of God's various faces,
so we do not know her
though we have seen her
everywhere—letting murder
happen, letting the cameras grind—
the one of us always
untouched, rejoicing, claiming
it is for the sake of love.

PRESERVES

In the neighborhood kitchens, aproned
women glide out of the banks of steam
bearing from hot stoves to countertops
kettles that boil up the stench of fruit.
Pectin, and the bricks of paraffin,
tumblers and jars ranked like canisters
under the windows, are implements
against the dead winter—the cellars
emptied and waiting, the harvest in.

There is no pleasure in our bounties
that is not deepened by woman's work;
clots of berries, apple peels unwound
off the serrations of tempered blades,
gouty plums—they melt over the flame,
pulps and syrups of purple and red
solemnly rendered through swollen cloth:
blood-colored jams, jellies that cloud
and congeal the light into a clean fire.

SPARROW HILLS

(After Boris Pasternak)

God, how my mouth swam
your nipples—Can't it be
like this forever? Endless
muggy summer, and night
after night the schmaltz
of that same accordion
we heard when we stood up
out of breath, slapping
the dust off our clothes?

People go queasy over time,
they make age scary as hell,
they talk all holy—you
don't fall for that drivel,
do you? You don't catch
nature on its knees praying;
the fields don't simper,
the ponds don't turn salty.
God doesn't care. Instead

let's crack our souls
wide open; today is all
time—the world's high noon;
use your eyes, look hard.
Whatever the two of us
touch turns to a muddle:
wood-birds, balsam, sky—
is it passion that colors
the pine spills like blood?

Forget the city; streetcars
stop miles from here, the woods
are trackless—anyway
nothing runs on Sundays.
We'll break down boughs
to rest on, play kid games
on the squirrel paths;
you slip on the needles,
I'll fall on top of you. . . .

God, the blindness of noon
this Sunday, being alone—
The woods say: this world
will never be civilized.
The pines believe in that,
and the wild fields—and so
should you. Here: hug me
under this crazy-quilt
the clouds unfold for us.

A LADY IN CHARCOAL

"It used to bother me," she says,
"How fickle the gods were, how they
Followed down woman after woman,
Brutal and indiscriminate,
siring demigods, breeding beasts
Too horrid for the world to bear;

It offended me, what they did.
I used to think: Poor foolish girls,
They had one glorious taste of love
And then it ended, and they starved.
They had a chance at heaven; heaven
Used them; heaven discarded them."

With the back of her hand she strokes
Her black cat's throat; she smiles sadly.
"Today," she says, "I am fifty-one;
All my mirrors give back my age.
I am closer to heaven than not,
So I think more kindly of the gods.

I see they are not to be blamed.
Now I remember how they connived
To love those women, how difficult
It was, the guises they were obliged
To wear. It was as if the women
Never wanted the gods to love them.

And of course they didn't. You see?
Even poor hungry Semele
Made her own selfish terms for love;
She was unbalanced, suicidal,
Sick. But the normal ones—they knew:
No woman can love the immortal.

Not that we don't wish to be cinders,
But that none of us can give love
Without sympathy; how can one
Feel passionately toward something
That will not die? Gods, and young men
Who have not begun to think of age,

We make fickle." She takes my hand;
The cat springs to the windowsill.
How does one answer such a speech?
She often talks like this to me,
To put me at ease, to tell me
I am always, always forgiven.

ONE-PART INVENTION

He offered me a month—simply as that.
He said: I'll give you a month with him,
one month. You won't be able to bear more.
Can you believe him, saying that? A man
who loves me? Can he love me so much?
Does he not love me at all—not know what
love is? Could you—to your own wife—
say: "I'll give you a month; then you'll be
tired of him?" No?

I'm cold—they have a door open somewhere.
What's the worst of it is
he's always right. A month. Less.
Two weeks. I think I can't love; I think
too much. Can you see? Is it the door?
Perhaps a window is open in the kitchen.

No, I believe in the psychotherapy,
but it hasn't worked for me—not yet.
It works for others; if I could find out
why I think, then it would work for me.
He isn't very good,
the man I go to. Three years: Nothing.
But you know, he becomes everything,
everything. Father, brother, lover.
You see, you relate to him; all you feel
goes out to him. And then . . .

You are old-fashioned. You blame me.
I admire your ignorance—you use it,
you make it work for you. Me
my ignorance devours.
Let's never mind. You admit all you know
of psychotherapy is what you've read
in the article about cats,
and what you learn from your own books.

Poor lucky you. But I do him good,
really. I'm the sort of wife has made him
stronger; he's had to be.
Behind every strong man is a sick woman?
You can imagine that—
and much more besides. You confess to
a difference between the woman your friend
and the woman you desire. What do you do?
You write, you listen to your records,
talk, drink coffee, smoke too much,
give a cocktail party every so often,
feel nostalgias that amuse you.

How we are restless together today!
Surely, he would give you a second month. . . .

MOTHER GOOSE IN A LATE AGE

Rain, rain, go to Spain

Yes, I can see myself clearly,
With a water-repellent coat
Flung on my arm. I am merely
A tourist strolling off the boat
At Málaga. Yes. I will say
That I saw Gibraltar and thought
It monumental. I will say,
Nonetheless, I would rather not
See it again. I will commit
Myself to the Spanish climate.
On the north-bound train I will sit
Alone, spending not much time at
Talk, except to admit I crave
Guitar, flamenco, olives, wine
And bullfights. And love. I will have
Love out of respect to some fine
Gypsy or Andalusian myth:
Rose in the teeth, dagger to breast,
Passions hotly to be met with,
Don Juans, duennas, all the rest.

I don't know anything of Spain,
But at Villacastín I'll meet
You for the winter. If your train
Is late from Paris, any street
Will serve for my impatient wait.
I'll walk fast, turn my collar up,
Curse the rain, snow, whatever state
The Spanish skies are in. I'll stop
In time to hurry back for you,

Only to find you had arrived
On time, and you had wandered, too,
A different way. If I had lived
Since Eden, to see you would be
No less exciting than the fall
Of those first lovers. After we
Trade our plain affections, and tell
Each other's trips, we will go back
To chart the streets. Beggars will find us
And importune us; a poor claque
Of urchins will chatter behind us.

We will drive up into the hills,
Take a small cottage for the year,
Make love in all weathers. There will
Be a blue lake, with water clear
As clear. At first the ice will blur
Its brilliance; we can only watch
Wild winter birds skimming the shore.
But spring will come; the cottage thatch
Will overgrow with flowers whose names,
Being Spanish, we will not know,
And the lake will melt in the flames
Of April's first hot sunrise. Oh,
I think then we will be in, by,
And on the lake a dozen hours
A day. You, underneath that sky
That drinks up its fire between showers,
Will be my Moorish beauty. I,
Anti-poet, will burn and peel.
Laugh at this dream, but I would die
To wake in Spain and have it real.

But I know nothing about Spain.
One year I lived in Germany,
And that was not the same. The plain
Truth is: There you never met me
With your blue coat beaded by rain
Or your gold scarf damp from snow
Or your brown hair straight, or the train
Windows unlidded by a row
Of scowling Spaniards looking out
To see if we were French. I know
Nothing of Spain—even about
A travel-folder Spain—and so
I made this up. But I suppose
It might have been something like this,
Foreign, with atmosphere I chose
Because it suits us. Our first kiss—
Think of it—changed the world of facts
Into nonsense. This might as well
Be nursery rhyme; it scarcely lacks
The faults of innocence to tell.

AFTER CARDS

"I have times when I live in a kind of constant
unreasoning fear of the next moment & the unknown,
times when I am sure nothing is predictable."
　　　　　　　　　　　　—a letter from a friend

We were sitting around
waiting for the sun to come up;
we had played poker all night
and now, four-thirty, some beer
left in the icebox, we sat
toting up gains and losses
and sipped from the wet cans.
The chips were sorted, the cards
heaped in the middle of the table.
Through the screened porch door
we heard the pond licking sand.
Nobody had lost much. Nobody
was in a hurry to drive home;
the host had promised breakfast,
an early swim. He had a boat
handy, if we wanted (he said)
a little old-fashioned angling
before we left; across the pond
in the shadows of the island
the crappies (he said) had been
hitting all week. Five-thirty
came on. In the lantern light
we polished off the beer, used
up the cigarettes, told jokes
and agreed how often we wished
we'd written down every damned one
of the good stories we'd heard
since adolescence. We cut cards
for quarters; we dealt around
a couple of hands of showdown;

we killed time. Six forty-five,
seven o'clock, and still no sun.
We sat, listening to the pond,
breathing the smell of kerosene.
Finally somebody said: *What about
that boat ride?* Then our host
got up, apologizing, and went off
into the dark to look for poles
and a flashlight, while the rest
of us argued who should go first.

RECLUSE

Lived not far from us,
corner of the county,
between here and the Kennebunks
where the fire in 'forty-seven
blacked the blueberry plains.
Kept cats—many as ten at a time.
Hiked up and down Old Mousam Road
before they made it macadam.
Used to look for tonic bottles,
picked devil's paint-brush.
Said: I do what I got to.
Said: I mind my own affairs.
Said: You do the same, son.
Said to him once: Hey,
you old Yankee bastard.
Answered: Shite, came from Kansas
sixty year ago. Said to him:
Hey, old Jayhawker bastard.
Smiled. Said: Hell, why not?
Said: Fire don't touch me,
nor drought nor rain neither.
Said: My chaff's good as
other people's wheat.
Dandelions boiled up thick,
blueberries and milk in July,
goldenrod for a garden,
daisies in a cracked pitcher.
Said: I paint my fences.
Laughed at him. Said to him:
Old farmer, what do you do,
who do you talk to,
what do you look ahead to?

Said to him: Ever get lonesome?
Snickered, turned around, said:
It's finished, son, all done.
Said to him: Meaning what?
Stopped, said: Trot off, son.
Said: Might sic the cats on you,
scratch you up for pure proudness.

BURNING OVER, COMING BACK

1.

At noon I took the boys
for a last walk through.
The field hadn't done right
by us the last three years;
bad luck, the dry summers,
or that we weren't natives
—no knowing why berries
scarce small as buckshot
were all Nature gave us,
why the fruit shriveled
and showed rust, and why
among the brittle leaves
what caught our eyes
was not the dust of blue
but patches of white web
some Maine spiders spun
to hold circles of dew.

We talked, my sons and I,
of the perversities
Nature lives by—how
to destroy this meadow
by our deliberate fire
was to ensure the crop,
the whole acreage to be
wax-green and indigo
for years. They took it as
magic: the hand of God
flaming on like a comic book
picture, refining evil

out of the low bushes
yet anonymous after the act.
I was the rationalist,
talking about chemistry
and ashes, arguing nothing
was certain in faith
—that we might forever be
obliged to buy blueberries
at the roadside stand
the other end of Harpswell.

We could burn it ourself,
said the youngest. His brother
scoffed: *But if we did,*
we might catch the trees
and wreck the old barn;
we're not like firemen,
not smart, not brave.

2.

The first two volunteers
came just at sunset
in an old black Dodge,
its paint turned purple oxide
on the skin; they brought
their wives and babies,
their dogs, their beer.
The pumper followed them,
wings of a scarlet horse
fading on its fat sides;

then came the rusted cars,
the antique motor-trucks:
Ford coupes with black boxes
in place of rumble-seats,
one Packard hearse
chopped off and boarded shut
behind the driver
—its curious somber bed
laid with brooms, shovels,
and in the cab two schoolboys
gaunt as young ghosts
who stood sour awhile
over their cans of ale.

The sowing of the fire
rustled at the meadow's end,
took root, grew. The men
in overalls strung out,
the mongrel dogs barked
after whatever creatures
the burning raised; we all,
juggling warm brew,
shouted our blue stories
into the loud precaution
of the pumper's engine.
In the night the flames
played on mothers' faces
and their children's;
seated on the fenders,
the hoods of the old cars,

families watched fathers
guarding with brooms
and broken evergreens
the burning perimeter—light
worrying the dark,
the dark re-forming itself
from the woods. All this
for blueberries,
to pleasure summer people.

3.

This house in winter stands
empty, the barn locked up,
the stony road to the highway
blocked with snow. Under
the wet drifts Nature
dreams on her ripeness
and feels in the spring thaw
a cleansing away of soot,
a readiness to be green.
Meanwhile the field burned;
I hugged my wife and sons
to watch the firemen
work in all our visions.
Oh, pies, the youngest whispered,
think of the pies next year,
when we come back.

THE MILITARY-INDUSTRIAL COMPLEX

On his free weekends he took
from its patent holster
the black sidearm, clicked
the safety off half-way
across the back lot, and sat
—we could see him, his legs
dangling over the edge of
the roof—sat on the hencoop.

After the first round or two
the chickens stayed inside
and gossiped the thunder
above their witless heads;
he would shoot, and the hens
echo, and another shell case
shine in the hot sun—the yard
a litter of brass and dung.

Flies. Green flies were what
he murdered from his perch,
brushing them from his face,
scowling them down to earth,
taking aim. He hammered them
into the dirt, into the wood
frame the wire was nailed to.
Hours this lasted—weekends.

At the start we had thought
it was the rats that raided
the coop from time to time—
and it all made sense: noise
and the panic of the fowl,

the killer in his khaki shirt
sitting at ease on the roof,
waving the sun from his eyes.

When it was not rats, we saw
this was none of our affair
and got used to it—weekdays
called him *Sir* and envied him
ribbons and rank. So what if
the chickens choked to death
on the spent casings, and men
working nights got no sleep?

A FEAR OF CHILDREN

She is as dainty as a Dresden doll
Primping. He is as enigmatic as
A wooden Swiss. The pink house they live in
Looks celluloid by day, coral by night;
Trellises of painted roses surround
A front door always shut. From chimney cap
To cornerstone, the neighbors are agreed
This house is the most durable of all.

On sultry summer nights the two withdraw
To the rear of the house. They sit, their feet
Dangling over the edge of the bedroom,
Their gaze tender on groves of sponge and wire.
They clap hands when an artificial wind
Refreshes them; they go to bed revived
And share in their synthetic innocence
Unsullied dreams skirting the fact of love.

Nightmares are accidental. If by chance
Their pretty bodies touch in the small bed,
Their heads fill up with horror, and the dreams
Go for the worse, ridden with grins and games.
Then they waken, sit upright, draw the sheets
Under their chins; they sigh, look sheepish, kiss.
She is as dainty as a Dresden doll.
He is as enigmatic as a Swiss.

AT NIGHT

It is day's end; I am thinking of weight—
how heavy I feel, how my flesh and my bones
having stayed alight so many hours are gone
all solemn like a cat slinking into a room.
The moon is outside the window, waning again;
it sits on its haunch in a circle of weather.
Tonight I am no brighter than the moon,
I only remember being silver and prophetic,
I move with no more haste than dark does.

Weight, I said. I find in you the pretense
of the moon—how you seem a center weathers
cleave to, how you assume a distant influence,
diminish but never fall, how you will not quite
disappear in the blackest night I invent you.
Instead—look—I am the one sinking, the one
worn, the one who feels even the moon's age
as near as the window it lights. Dull gravity—
tonight a thousand moons won't make me flow.

And at morning when this moon low in the west
looks to be etched in glass, then it will twin
you and be like half a dream. I may not bear
the weight of you, you are all a coursing on
the Zodiac from one sterile sign to the next,
you are the sea creature I cannot begin to coax
to the lap of the earth—whose close approach
would heave up houses. This is an invention of
bodies and forces, of fatigue and sleeping alone.

THE ROCKING CHAIR

It is a dream absolutely
wordless, and lasts the night—
like a habit of the ocean,
the moon on a varnished hull.

A man in the chair is going
nowhere, and in his lap rides
a woman, dressed in white,
hugging his bowsprit neck,

rocking, rocking, rocking
over the dream's tidy waves.
I know I am the man in this,
can feel pleasure whisper

through my whole mind; it is
shore wind in a bare rigging,
it breathes through my body,
I have never slept deeper.

The woman's face is sunk
deep in the reefs of my bones,
covert in her own loosed hair,
and she has no mortal weight

for she is namesake, symbol,
my figurehead forerunning love.
We float at anchor; we sway
in the lee world all night.

THE PERSISTENCE OF DESIRE

On a Sunday in August the lovers
are in the kitchen. He is sitting
in a painted chair; she is cutting
his hair with her mother's shears.

She has robed him in a blue towel
and moves around and around while
his soft hair drifts to the linoleum.
She is careful, liking his hair long.

She has set out her father's whisky,
the bottle is open nearby. Already
he is a little drunk. She is not:
her hand is steady, her eye clear.

Later in the yard they will shake
the loose clippings over the lawn.
They will rest on the dark porch,
the blue towel under their heads,

the neighborhood windows seeming
like shop-fronts lighted all year.

BONE

We will imagine for the time
being she has discovered it
in Africa, a continent
whereon its unaccustomed white

leapt to her eye, and let us say
that reaching after it her hand
encounters such oddness of shape
she cannot tell if beast or man

was made with it. The bone is small
and winged, no thicker than an inch,
hollowed through as if the ring
around a cylinder of flesh

long since decayed. *Marrow,* she thinks.
and puts the relic in her purse.
There it stays. At the customs desk
turning it out she is at first

embarrassed; vertebral and stark
it lies among her coins, the clerk
is curious, he fingers it.
She tells him she will have it worked

into a costume piece, hurries
to hide the object from his sight.
Coming home to America
she keeps it to herself. At night

she lies awake to study it;
by day she makes its surface smooth
with fondling. Girlish symbolist,
she names it Love, and with her mouth

shaped in a kiss she traces it;
it kisses back—bloodless, thus chaste.
Marrow, she thinks, *of what?* and finds
she does not care if man or beast.

THE MARAUDER

When they shot the bear out of his tree,
North, on Monday, in Cedar County,
It occurred to us the bear knew, too,
Something was not enough—a stirring,
A yearning for sweetness buried deep
In the shrunk gut, portentous forage.
We knew and he knew: it was something
Not to perish of capture, sloven
And soft from caramel corn, smarting
With mange under the fur, with cinders
Lodged in the cracked pads. Something—at least
Not a cage—but not, truly, enough.
When they shot the bear out of his tree,
A single shot, and the limber trunk
Yawed with the target, sprang back, sang out
As green wood does in the springtime, stopped—
When the bear chose to drop, swam the air
Littered by yellow buds, pulled with him
The slim top twigs to the populous
Field—the tree bled; the earth at its roots
Shook and the worms far under felt: waking.
For them, too, not enough, but something.

WEEKENDS AT THE COVE

Here is an old seal sleeps
Like a rock, dun as mud, dull
As the bottom of the summer.
Coming back from a Sunday sail
You see him, brown bulk in the sun,
Think you hear him snoring—some noise
Lower than the wind in pale birches—
Point him out to the smart visitors.

Fat landmark on the foam-humped shore,
He might be a century old, might
Bear weathers and scars distance heals,
Might even be dead, kept by stark salt
But monumental like the stone-falls
That are abutments on high water—
And so you kneel and scour the deck
For bottle caps to pelt him with.

These break and shine across the air,
Some short, some true as a circle knows.
Grudging the grace of weighty things
The seal moves, lives, makes for the sea;
Where he goes down is a gold shadow
Failing in the wake of your shouts,
And the many Sundays you sail after
Will not raise him again.

ON NOT KNOWING THE NAMES
OF THE FLOWERS IN MONTANA

Look at these fields. They are miles of purple
Modest spires like a far city at dusk
Filling the valleys of a destination,
They are such color as the mind rides on,
They blow in a south wind we name *yesterday*.

On both sides of us yellow scarves unfurl
The road; they are jetsam of wagon trains,
Pretty Hartford ladies trailing and losing
From their thin fingers whatever civilized
Their carriage in the canyons of the East.

Up the green rake of mountains, where the eye
Waters and the heart makes much of its work,
A thousand wings of white flutter and swim
Out of the grass; they are moths, numerous moths,
And blue bees scavenge them in the hot light.

Even at the highest reaches of sight
Where no trees stand, and stone like layers of cloud
Shows what the world is, the snowfields are pink
And melt downward into their water-trails
Petals whose perfect roundness measures time.

This West is whole color. Now we must find
Some native to inquire the names earth takes
On the hard slopes where no one wants to live;
Now we wind down in the chilly shade, wanting
Places to sleep where even the rocks are flowers.

THE SUSPENSE OF MEETING

He reads the face of his watch,
Ticks the coffee cup with a spoon,
Sends his dreams out the plate-
Glass window to ride with strangers
In their warm cars to fetch her.

Wherever she is, she is not
In the company of time; time is
With him, and engages him quite.
He smokes the solemn quarter-hours;
The cloud on the restaurant glass

Is where he draws out her name
To amuse the humorless minutes;
The empty matchbook his fingers
Reduce to tatters is impatience
Counted into ragged seconds.

Wherever she is, she is deathless,
Safe from blood and the mundane
Clockwork of desire. Love, traffic,
This cold day leading to spring—now
He feels guilty for wanting her

Faster than he needs her here
In this public place, and just now
Seeing her wave from the street
He knows he has asked her to grow
Older for him, and she has said Yes.

THE MOZART BROADCAST

"An agony of flame that cannot singe a sleeve."
—W. B. Yeats

1.

In the hundred miles between
the concert hall and this room
millions are listening in;
it ought to seem to them
they are no more deprived
than the patrons in the seats
who doze, who have arrived
after rich luncheons, who meet
week after week their peers
up and down the scarlet aisles,
who have held tickets for years.
Yet only this hundred miles
makes a crucial difference:
reaches of dour cumulus,
ionic drift, the chance
intervention of hills
whose altitudes impede
signal—there is no recourse
from Nature. The rains bead
the window, lightning is Morse
encrypting the text, the source
fades and returns no more
true than if the world's worst
leader read out the score.
Like every remote hearer
we huddle before the dial,
but bring Mozart no nearer
than the same hundred miles.

2.

It is distance
obsesses us, of one sort
or other—the miles
of this or that ocean
seem, though measurable,
nevertheless trebled
by our attention.

If sound were solid,
able to cast on the walls
shadows so as to be,
like our other pleasures,
real—*sculpture; love*—
we could endure
any prodigious space.

Since it is not,
we are half-mute, float
helplessly adrift,
while the program we hoped
would save us falters.
Hear it: technicians
call it "white noise."

I wish we might stay
forever in this twilight,
our hands linked,
explaining to ourselves
how even the things
no one can touch
we define sensually.

3.

We wait for our last Monday,
survive the tedious weekend—
yesterday with its lethargies,
Sunday with its eternal
electric querulous weathers.

I am sure, looking at you
as one looks at the paintings
of jugs and alizarin apples
the supplements reproduce,
how art falsifies sense;

stay close to me. We must tune
whatever nerves give us access,
loosen certain frets, devise
embouchures and fingerings
suited to these brief passages.

Listen to the music, listen
to the radio's crackle and hiss;
the disturbances of summer
catch us into the overture.
Behind us the doors go shut.

The dark room is all whispers,
the air weighty, the rain over;
we are the last latecomers
ushered in, and the wetness
of our coats freshens the hall.

OCTOBER

All we think about
is a distraction
strung out in the mind
like flocks of black
geese on the flyways
that lead southward
this month, like a high
calling to the body.
Our thoughts, our silly
geese, cry purposes
above the wicked smoke
the northern cities
make of the landscape;
they are a wishful
pattern, out of reach
but wheeling closer
to settle the marshes
where they are clumsy.
We track them, not
to make a game of them
but to see them real,
every feather to be
a glitter of beads.
What cuts to our bones
is a wind from Canada;
in our wild thoughts
is a rabble of wings
rising to bear us both
to Mexicos of love.

THREE DREAMS

1.

I am walking along a sandy shore
by myself, looking into the lake;
in its brown depths I begin to see
fish, all sizes. I feel pleasure
at first, and then dismay, for all
of them float motionless, rigid,
all dead just under the surface.

2.

A place to recover. But my ease
in the cool shade of the birches,
my joy in the small white flowers
underfoot—these vanish in a moment:
the ground is all at once bare, cans
and green bottles litter the woods.
I find myself at the brink of a pit.

Now I am looking down on the colors
of a different death—browns, yellows,
grays and blacks, whites and oranges.
This is a grave of kittens; they are
stacked like firewood, they have not
begun to decay, they are the pets
of a hundred children who mourn them.

3.

Then you appear, magically, a child
holding each of your hands; a smile
begins when you see me. I meet you,
I say: Come witness these horrible,
horrible things. I show you the fish.
As we watch, they flex, turn upright
and swim away in the dark water.

I take you to the kittens' graveyard,
and of course you and your children
kneel at the edge to pick up, one
by one, the tiny, squirming animals;
I hear them mewing, hear the laughter
of your children. You say to me:
You must expect things to be changed.

THE OPERA

I regret going back
to old places—the streets
that are made into freeways,
the plazas and airfields
named after great men who
were alive when we loved.

It is as if by stopping
our attentions to each other
we set something heartless
in motion—that you re-did
the world, that I altered
its common names to hide you.

Now you are lost to me,
I believe I never took you
to hear Rimsky-Korsakov—
you wearing your white dress
with the hot orange shapes
I called kisses-in-the-snow.

FARM POND

The pond forgets its pleasures.
The rain traces circles of touch
until the pond-skin shivers, yet
a moment after the rain has quit
the pond's blank as a fool. Every-
thing, for ponds, is the first time.

THE ANIMALS

When they are
underfoot we tolerate them;
they are stupid
but docile enough.

We invent them
good intentions—they adore
children; they are warm
at the foot of the bed.

If they are noisy
it is because they miss
home, or whimper
for lost brothers;

we make a community
with them. And when
they lick our hands
for salt,

or follow us for food,
or lie dozing
against our legs at dark,
we talk to them as if

they understood. We
are weighty with love
we cannot articulate
for them, nor they for us.

Our lives are dumb
show—the sensual engagement
of our flesh with fur
and claw, with rough tongues

43

we take to be instruments
of kisses. O animals!
We cannot disbelieve in
their souls;

we cannot fault
the innocence of their eyes.
If they kill,
it is from a need

whose portents we are not
privy to; if they are cruel,
they obey laws
we are too civil to heed;

we excuse them by habit.
By habit
we are a fond accomplice
to their Nature.

THE PLOT TO BLOW UP NEW HAVEN

All night I watch you
asleep, scarcely able to make of
you anything but a ghost—
yet I imagine I am
holding your hand; I imagine
I hear you breathe;
I imagine (because I believe in
nothing) I am free to kiss you
with no fear while your apparition
sifts, like smoke
through chunk-holed windows,
into my lungs to haunt me.
Believing in your ghost,
I am not afraid to be
possessed; and I am willing
to make you carnal.

In the street a truck
passes, and this old house shivers.
Containing you, I burn
like an engine firing white gas;
we drift inseparably
out of the room on the cool exhaust
from last night's traffic
and ride disguised as a cloud
over the jails, banks,
churches. You operate inside me,
a conscience
energetic as angels. Streetlights
cast our single shadow,
which stretches and curls
and makes figures on the pavement for
black children to trace.

All night I have this
dream—until the slow coming-alive
of the sunrise begins
in the narrow space between the shade
and the window-frame.
I open your closet door to block it—
the light slides around and over,
touches your face, draws
features and dimensions, colors
the silence we lie in,
shows me armatures of your body
moulded under the bedclothes.
Light empties me, turns you
to your own flesh, fills craze-lines
in the plaster, repeats
the rails of the headboard.

Now you wake up and we hug
each other, we feel the city
moving, talking, we count it:
the rhythm of our hearts.
The secret ghosts of us open
huge eyes behind the lattices of
their adjacent cells
and sing—they rehearse plots
to save the world from itself
by explosion. My white love,
my spirit real as a cloud,
my second self: the city
ignites from this tinderbox room
and claims us victims.
New Haven, you
are already kindling.

ARMATURES

1.

In hot weather
bones sweat
as flesh does.
In winter
shiver, like
the figures
informed by them.
In spring they
are jubilant,
do humorous dances
and are green.
At first frost
they put on
like field animals
a camouflage,
and by snowfall
are invisible.

2.

A lover might say
to his lady
that his love is
the bleached rib-cage
some desert beast
once had a heart in:

an emotion clean as
the moon,
a cage to be gladly
caught in, a bower
whose regular shadows
define his days

47

and his white nights;
he might fancy
the experience of love
like alternatives,
and its music worn
xylophones.

3.
If I were building a house
in a graveyard
I would claim the old bones
as my own; I would say
to the contractor:
Damn you if you steal one bone.
I would build a fireplace
from the weathered markers
and pass winter evenings
reading the names of the dead.
I would go to a greenhouse
to discover which fruit trees
I shall set in; I pray
limes.

If I were building a house
in a graveyard
I would invite lovers to lie
under my windows
and old men who remember war
to bring me bronze flags
and mothers who were mothers
for nothing
to lay wreaths at my door.

GEODE

They said to him:
Why do you live inside
a stone? because
you like to live alone?
are you frightened?
isn't there anyone
inside with you?

And no one was.
But he never came out
(though he could hear
through damp walls the shouts
outsiders made)
and not one of them dared
go in with him.

He told himself:
Nothing is wrong with me
if I prefer
a private way of life;
I've light enough
for what I want to see
without windows.

This was the truth.
He had a crystal world
of white and gold,
one bedroom like a star
to grow old in,
a climate for his dreams
constant and cold.

They said to him:
Come out and talk to us;
what do you eat?
where do you make your waste?
what do you wear?
are you too weak to face
the likes of us?

He told them No,
and slept all by himself
curled on the stones
he ate and drank; he kept
his own counsel;
he shored his bones against
their hammers.

US AND THE ANIMALS

We eat the eggs of birds
and the flanks of solemn cows
and the delicate brains of
lambs thinking fleece and flowers.
What's the point of us, love?
Seeing what we share of lives
animals live, what's the natural
consequence of lying together
if not a dumb dependence
of flesh on unclothed flesh?

O the flowers with white hats
and the wind that lifts them . . .
the stiff grasses crushed flat . . .
the tracks our bodies lie on
being the path to a shut gate
unused across twenty years . . .
the hot, dry song of locusts
blurring the irrelevant sun . . .
Love, we say, *love*, waiting here
for nightfall and the herds
in the next meadow to move home.

"I KNOW I WILL WEEP FOREVER"

For Peg Mullen

The pieces of men
are picked from the field
into plastic bags, slung
between the shoulders
shrugged by the living
under bamboo poles cut
for this kind of work.

The bags are sorted
and iced like any flesh
for distant shipment.
They are consigned
to airports; they are
addressed to outlets
new in the business.

O on the continents
a dateline apart, soldiers
sweat; the job gives
no holidays for sorrow;
armies are frantic
to supply the mothers
not yet shipped to.

THE BLACK CAT

For the time it takes me
to smoke a cigarette
I have prowled this house.
My wife in the big bed
lies cradling my pillow
in the bow of her arms,
and she has no dream
that excludes me. My younger
son has withdrawn himself
to a far corner of the dark
breathing untroubled music.
My older son, the distant me
I remember over and over,
raises himself to kiss me
while I settle his covers
between repose and the wind.
Even the family cat dozes
in the rocker, his claws
unsheathed into the cushion.
What hurried me home
to them all was the absurd
fear they were murdered.
Some blind animal lunged
into my loneliness
and showed itself: *Death,*
I whispered, calling the beast
by the most exciting name
I could think of. Now
feeling foolish and tired
I have ended my round
to learn nothing but love.
I read too much, perhaps,

or wish the wrong liberties,
but I will sit for hours
at the window where light
enters first, hurt by guilt
and relief to watch the cat
go killing in his sleep.

HANGING CURTAINS:
VARIATIONS ON A THEME OF TOLSTOY

1.

Every husband knows
the bareness of a room
with nothing at the windows:
appetites are too plain,
the partners brazen,
and the eyes looking in
increasingly amazed.

To love in a new house
is to seem to furnish it
—the carpets first,
certain upholstered pieces,
sentimental bric-a-brac,
the curtains last of all.

But nothing is hidden.
Under the rugs: floorboards.
Behind the sofa: walls.
On the other side of curtains
the light is hard
and dust-motes idle in it.

By night the partners
pretend it is pleasure
they give each other.
The husband knows: the curtains
hold warmth neither in nor out,
and they hold the years
neither in nor out.

2.

Falling, he sees
the curtains are askew.

The ladder represents
ambition, perhaps,
or children on whose concern
he ought to be borne
past middle age,
or only a way toward love

If he does not get up,
climb the rungs,
adjust the new curtains,
someone may spy in.

What is the answer to the eyes?

It is to climb chairbacks
when you have no ladder;
to put curtains up
and take them down;
to move continuously
into new houses, new rooms
where the floorboards curl
and the window glass
ripples like water.

3.

The husband dreams.

He is in a room
stripped of its furnishings,
lying on a thin mattress,
staring up at the window.

The white curtains
are an angel on a ladder
leaned against the wind.

On the far side of the glass:
darkness.
The angel raises the sash
to its widest opening
and the dark flows inside.

The dreamer puts up his hand;
the darkness rises
to his elbow, to his wrist.

He tries to reach the ladder.
He wishes the angel to take his hand.
He hopes he will float on the dark
over the windowsill,
and he imagines he will seize
the curtains on the way past.

He believes
he will catch the angel
on the way past.

BOUNDARIES

Outside, the fog is
marching through the black
barricades of bare maples,
crystals of snow
are marching
down the cold highway
of the wind,
and yellow light is
marching in the squares
windows build on the night;
in the back yard
the gentle rabbits
are marching through
the barren garden;
overhead the blind clouds
are marching, the stars
and the imagined moon
are marching the universe.
The man in the warm bed
is not marching.
His mind turns
the marching over and over
and tells him it is
his heart he hears,
the dresser clock,
the drumming of the furnace
at the bottom of the house.

The window is open
and the world is hollow:
the far-off whine of trucks
—are the trucks marching?—

is as near as
the ticking of his watch
under the pillow;
he hears the groaning
of a train which may be
ten miles away, in the next
county, its solemn whistle
amplified by fog
and the chances of the wind,
and he cannot tell
which way the train is
marching on its steel tracks.

Now he would prefer
to fall asleep,
but his watch is marching
around and around
his wrist, and his pulse
is marching up and down
the vulnerable lengths
of his body, and now he thinks
how the locks
are marching from door to door
carrying their keys
like knives with ugly
serrations along their edges,
how the trucks far off
are painted red and their
drivers shiver marching
over every crack in the pavement,
how the trains
are marching under the freight
of a thousand armed men,

how the fog conceals
its own marching
and the rabbits contrive
to put on white and move
without a sound
so that only their tracks
go marching and marching
at the boundaries
of the little land he owns.

He lies on his side
in the warm bed, listening
to the message of his watch;
he thinks he will empty
his pillowcase,
fill it with rations enough
to live on for a month,
unfurl the broad sheets
under him into a flag
even the rabbits
can rally to, gather the locks
and the wicked keys
to himself, follow
the hall nightlight
through the dark fears
of his life until he is free,
and able at last to sleep.

A LITERARY LESSON

For the lady's memory

Twenty years ago I said
to Elizabeth Bowen
"May we have tea together?"

and she answered me "Oh, yes,"
the soul of her smile dancing,
"that would be" holding each word

like an object "delightful"
—because she stammered but knew
how to master speech by hang-

ing on until she tamed it—
so we sat out of the wind
at our literary drink,

Elizabeth's careful words
teaching me to love patience.

THE KINGDOM OF THE ORDINARY

The king nods on his throne, the sun
is not quite round at his window,
his queen makes clatter in the kitchen:
pickles from her own cucumbers.

It is a hard case, this shadowing
the state undergoes in castle rooms,
for one must rule the day, grant it
fair audience, and write its laws.

The laws are difficult; what king
can spend a whole life making them—
brittle but just, and so refined
as to imitate hunger and love—

if the daily rebellion shakes him
and he cares how it all comes out?

MOVING BACK

Comfort is nothing, I said,
believing I had forgot
all of that: love, clocks,
butter, and the train to work;
the quarrels of the children
insisting Wake up, Wake up;
the warm bed, the carpets.

How natural to know peace.
I said that; I believed it
for a week—but the slow owls
no matter how they ponder
can think only of mice,
and in the short afternoons
branches break of themselves.

I might have bought a rifle
to take aim at the white sun,
or a rope, to set my snares
wherever the tracks appeared;
or an axe—to sharpen it,
to mark the trunks of the pines,
to call the thick pitch blood.

THE WEDDING RING

She finds it in random places:
next to his empty coffee cup,
on the bench in the garage,
behind the bathroom faucets.
When she chides him he shrugs
and twists it lightly back on.
Mothers to their daughters say
how the ring finger is chosen,
how the thin channels of blood
flow straight into the heart,
how the heartbeat in the ring
teaches the partners fidelity.
Only superstition, she thinks;
in her bones the very marrow
drums for marriage and a love
beyond old wives' tales passed
to new brides. But she frets:

O love, she thinks, was this
a marriage too dependent upon
its props and its cold facts?
The ring was an extravagance
and a festivity, to celebrate
our ownership of one another;
I wanted the ladies who met
and desired you to remember
whose man you were—thereby,

as they satisfied themselves,
to deepen the luxury learned
in your embrace; and deepen
the sorrow, too. I imagined
each tired mistress kissing
your fingers in the darkness,
knowing the taste of my ring
and honoring me with her hurt.

That too might be a pleasure,
she thinks, of a certain kind.
Much better if he came to her
one night as she half slept,
waiting for him by dreaming on
a daughter of her own blood—
came to her like the shadows
of all men who make contracts
thoughtlessly in their youth,
saying: I've lost your ring;
I forget its old symbolism;
wherever I misplaced it last
it has melted into the world
of our possessions and it is
meaningless, though everything
we own shines brighter now
and is finally precious to me.

A WOMAN

I never get enough of love.
Never enough. And lacking it
I pace, I kick the furniture.
One night I broke the handle off
A teacup, and stepped on the dish.

Why do you stay away from me?
My God, what do you think is worth
The wishing for, outside this room?
My windows are mirrors at night;
Rain after dark makes me a freak.

Do you know what I'd like to be?
One of those ugly plants with pods
Hanging off them. I'd love to watch
My body wither, and the pods split,
And all the seeds come breaking out.

SUNDAY AT THE SHORE

We sit by the sea. I tell you
how I am absorbed in the women
squatting on blankets in the sun.
You laugh at me, as if the women
were nothing to you. At noon,
at that time of day most bleak
because shadowless, we swelter
on the sand and talk, idly,
about lunch or one final swim.

Most of the women are mothers.
I try to imagine them younger,
childless—not even married,
perhaps. Then they were slimmer,
were not embarrassed on the beach
(looking at men, sullen, annoyed
because the men are not watching),
were at ease with what they wore.

It is odd, I try to tell you,
how we are filled with affection
for things dying: a pleasure
perverse as parting from friends
we know we will never see again.
I try to explain to you—how
a man stares at tired mothers
and covets the maidens he sees.

What is it lies at the center
of the life we lead? I say,
and you scarcely listen, it is
to love everyone we can,

even to be promiscuous
if we learn no satisfaction
from fidelity; that it is
a sin to be celibate. I say
the very body that covered you
last night is a different flesh

than you will support tonight.
I say, sprinkling white sand
the tanned length of your arms,
body is all kinds of vehicle
laden with the usual freight.
The destinations are changeless:
where the mind lives, places
tracks lead to in both of us,
dingy warehouses piling up
our heavy sexual commerce.

I must go on to explain
how in the first strange moment
of arrival at this beach
beauty was all around me—
not of the mothers fretful
over their children, nor green
water, lit by the white buoys
and the white bathing caps,
nor of the dimmed horizons,

but of what among my thoughts
is *déjà vu,* this fixed circle
comprising color and youth,
earth and water and clear air,

this composed world gardening
the steamy flowers of desire.
When I tell you this vision,
as commonplace as the heat
rippling upward from the sand,

it is, you think, a distortion
inappropriate to Nature.
But Nature too, in her own
shapes is transient. Tomorrow
we will come back and lie
on the coarse humid sugar
of this shore. Will you admit
nothing is quite familiar?
Nothing is exactly the same?

Tomorrow. Meanwhile we sit
without eating, hour on hour,
dry-lunged, fat with boredom.
The sun closes its circle
and the swimmers call softly.
Like brooding yellow willows
all the mothers are lovely
with the love brimming my mind,
hunched over drowsy infants
to give a pretense of shade.

DEMON LOVERS

You said: I know
I am mad in one room
of my mind,
but I never visit there
without shutting the door.
The rest of the house
runs as usual;
the whole neighborhood
is ignorant; tradesmen
make their ordinary calls.

But it is my room,
I told you. You shrieked
like a child,
fell against me
with your empty hands
hard as talons on my back.
I saw your eyes
through the closed lids
like blue stones,
and heard you cursing love.

THE DESIRE FOR SERVANTS

Time and again the birds intrude
through windows left open—
rasping, beating their wings,
plumaged with light flown in
from the yard where the cat
I am sure is a trial to them.

I find them clinging to the lace
of the parlor curtains,
their eyes brilliant with wildness
and their small mottled heads
jerking like frames of film
on the white screen of afternoon.

It is no good talking to them.
Their language is too private
and their visions so broad
they cannot fix me a place
except as a predator—
they implicate me in their fright.

And, finally, in their death; next day
the delicate figures
lie in a ring of feathers
under the snare-shadows
my curtains make on them.
I live alone; what's to be done?

If there were others in the house
to summon—persons to whom
a man might say: *Look here!*—
whose hours and instruments
waited on my discretions,
I might then delegate myself,

ordering the cat locked upstairs,
a disinfectant fetched,
gloves and a shoebox sent for,
requiring of these persons
that nothing be seen to
until I had gone from the room.

Instead I take up by one claw
a slight, dense weight that tugs
muscles I rarely use,
that sets to work the engine
whose dry traffic ascends
the bare twigs of my own fear.

IT IS NOTHING TO LIVE ALONE

When the body is tired, it sleeps;
When it is not, it works—it goes
To closets and to bureau drawers,
It finds clothing, dresses itself,
Performs and functions, drinks and eats.
The body turns on television
And seats itself in front of it;
It lets in the cat and puts down food.
Is is nothing to live alone.

At noon, before the kitchen window,
I watch outside. The yard is bare.
The killed lawn keeps a yellow cast
As if it hugged, inside, its green.
The poplars are stark, the willow stripped;
I think, in the clutter of my kitchen:
No tree is more forlorn than that one.
It follows that I am fond of the willow
And regret the leaves strewn under it.

By four o'clock the sun is gone;
I am surprised not to miss it
And charge that to the proprieties
Of the season. Blue clouds are building
Westward; people are dying, there,
And most of them will die lonely.
Like my willow, they are mourned too late—
But it is nothing to live alone:
When the body is tired, it sleeps.

SOMETHING OF LOVE

I remember we were driving
in your mother's old blue Chevy;
it was near three in the morning,
summer, the sun still far below
the horizon but morning birds
beginning to creak and whirr like
familiar comfortable machines
in an unheated shed. I rolled
the windows down; the damp air
smelled contradictory and green.
We had left the cemetery
where we knew all the gravel roads,
every bronze flag and flower pot,
every faucet leaking to be
St. Francis for thirsty squirrels;
we had played all night—nothing
serious—on the slant of lawn
by the mausoleum, the house
with no one home, mussing ourselves,
laughing that someone's ancestors
were clenching bony hands, saying
frantic prayers in whispers cold
as wind under a broken door.
Between our sweet lives and death
was immovable Nature—its roots,
weeds, insoluble masonries;
sweaty and quick we had hugged,
melted into each other's clothes
pretending to manufacture
children who might witness to us.
Now we shook off the print of grass,

the temperature of earth, even
the shamefaced cemetery ghosts.
Love, I said, *oh love, oh good love,*
how I hurt for you and from you.
That was true: It hurt to breathe,
hurt to put my foot to the brake,
hurt me to turn the wheel; it hurt
when I inhaled a cigarette,
and if I coughed I died. You said:
Oh dear dearest darling, what can I do?
So I told you, and stopped the car
on Laurel, this side of the old
tennis courts, and you did it. *Love.*

We never accustom ourselves
to love's lineaments. Woman, wife,
mother, lover too good for me —
that was twenty-five years ago.
How many flowers we have brought
to our parents, how many cars
we have bought and traded away. . . .
We have manufactured real sons,
have felt the space separating
us from the underworld shrink (roots
withering and letting go, earth
washing away, spring after spring),
hear — louder and louder — voices
under the doors of every house
we live in. The best of it is:
Now we are always close together —
so close that I have noticed how
when I do something important

you are suddenly in my way
and are part of the importance.
How I love to quarrel with you,
to swing in your rage as if in
some hammock under bending trees;
how I love to put on your scorn
like a coat I cannot make fit;
how I love your kindness, which sits
close to my face, curling its paws,
and makes me tremble with purring;
how I love your patience—it is
a children's orchestra waiting
to be told what to play. *Oh dear*
dearest darling, what can I do?
And I tell you, and stop the car
on Laurel, this side of the old
tennis courts, and you do it, *love*.
Then when I start the car we drive
away from the graveyards, forever.

THE IMMORTALIST

If you were to follow him in and out of life,
his life, day after day, you would be struck to find
that he finishes nothing. Find a coffee cup
he has drunk from; cold coffee, a half-inch of it,
sits in the bottom of the cup. The chances are
some time has passed since he poured it; wonderful plants
proliferate out of the black; alive gray spores
suck up the drink and lie hideously awake.

In his kitchen, bedroom, bathroom, and living-room
—wherever there are ashtrays of whatever shapes—
hardly-smoked cigarettes collect, some of them burnt
tip to tip leaving the bare ash solemn and whole
like moulted fire-dragons from a Chinese egg,
the rest half-wasted, balanced on a rim of glass
inside the paper collar their last heat hunched in.
He smokes endlessly, yet he scarcely smokes at all.

He has women. You can walk the streets anywhere
and figure to yourself that half the girls you meet
were, one time, his—all in the special way he has,
which is not quite to possess them, but to make threats
in a language indistinguishable from love's
and in gestures any woman recognizes
until it is too late for her to tell him *yes*.
By then he is not listening; by then he is gone.

Everything. Everything. The same arrest, the same
disjunction, the same *no*. You cannot understand
why he reads books only part-through, and will not stay
to the end of movies; the inside record grooves

of his collection are unworn, he has not learned
a single poem by heart, he does not eat desserts.
You wonder who he is, never to finish with—
and, if this pleases him, what he will not come to. . . .

THE EMIGRÉ

Sergei Yesenin, 1895–1925

I dream now and again of youngish girls
Cloaked in the dark plumage of leotards—
How their puffed pudenda bow and withdraw
Between the muscular wings of their thighs.
They cross my mind like some great neckless birds,
These dancers, migrating at dizzying height
All up and down the flyways of my thoughts,
Searching the paradise of melting lakes.

Thrumming in sweet cadence across my brow,
Their inspired flight turns music in my brain;
They baffle my tired lids. I shut my eyes
To the seasons and their far silhouettes;
I will not think of them, ghosts carnal in
My dreams and nearly real in memories,
But I write them and make their bodies poems—
And so, comrades, we touch one another.

This month the birches of Russia must be
Foliaged with the restless shapes of birds
Whose song is the fervor of her new age—
Yet it is a cold spring in that hard world.
On the half-forgot farm of my childhood
The sun tumbles like snow through the white trees;
it falls upon dull, humble animals,
And the peasant girls, watching by, shiver.

Much oftener than before I get drunk
On profusion—of wings and limbs and leaves
Snarled between me and desirable light.
I remember the graceful birches cast

Blue shadows on the bosoms of the girls;
When we are young all color is so pure—
Deep as the thin veins beating at my wrist
The disingenuous metrics of return.

THE FOLLY OF POETRY

Jackson State & Kent State: 1970

He had a dream, a vision of some confusion
that came to him in the dark in a windstorm,
intermittently performed behind curtains
lightning made. The actors' faces moved
like lanterns in a garden, and their hands
gestured into the wind like bare branches,
and the voices of the actors were reflections
of light playing at the edges of new marble,
saying to the dreamer: "Write us down, name
our names, remember us, keep us alive to nag
the cops who hate niggers, the good soldiers
who are scared of kids; write us down again,
make us immortal." And the dreamer replied:
"This is a dream, and the six of you likewise
are a dream within a dream, and the years
will pass which are also a dream—and what
can be made of that?" And the actors said:
"What is real?" And the dreamer, he embraced
his pillow and said: "I don't know anything
about it." And the six children held hands
in the lightning and laughed and cried out,
and said: "Write us down anyway, for the hell
of it." And the dreamer imagined he knew
something about hell, and then, like a man
talking to a girl he loved when he was young,
the dreamer said into his pillow: "I can't
forget you; how can anyone ever forget you,
year after year, army after army?" "Then,"
said the six actors in the storm and wind,
"write us down." And the dreamer said: "No.
In a bad dream, in a nightmare which comes

81

over and over again, in a shadow country
where no one learns anything about reality,
it is no help for us to write anything down."
And he woke up in the dark, and the dream
and the lightning woke up alongside him.

ENDSONG

It's going to be a hard winter.
Look through the almanac, look
at the coat of the caterpillar,
look in the window-well where
the cat has stockpiled mice—
fieldmice, a half dozen of them,
mingled with leaves from poplars
whose nakedness offends the wind.

Wherever you look, the portents
bear the same burden: it's going
to be a hard winter, the lawns
will mold under the deep drifts,
the greens will thirst to death
in their dry dirt—are brown
already with a chill foresight;
look at the puffy, bundled spruce.

Look at the words of your love,
inside the envelope look,
read, believe in the weathers
she promises. If your cheeks
burn, it is not the heart's fever
but the sting out of the north,
excoriations of early snow—
the hard winter it's going to be.

PERSONS

*It is almost
Embarrassing to be alive alone.*
—W. S. Graham

This morning I am early into the kitchen,
make coffee, orange juice, put down milk
for the cat. Overnight a fog has settled:
loneliness confirms it; the cottonwood is
my spirit stretching all its long bones
and the shades of four birds are pleasures
set at the highest end of my reaching out.

I am thinking of you. It is the first joy
of being alive in this house that nothing
keeps me from you; my mind spirals and slides
as on blue air, it touches stem or wire,
it is damp on the feathers of the birds,
a cloud from the teakettle, the garnet color
of coffee. All the world partakes of you.

Probably I had thought of you in my sleep.
Waking to the half light through the curtains
I sensed the black cat near my face hunting
in his dreams, the furnace silent. O you!
Like something wonderful flown off, you are
more vivid by your absence. This cat, blind
after years of sight, knows what it is I mean.

I am waiting for you, witness at this window—
the natural world obscured, the four tall birds
gone, the cat finding out, certain, his path to
the white saucer. Only you are you. Language,
I learn, serves for more than telling weathers,
but like wings opening light it discovers you,
second person, best pleasure of waking alone.

THE CALL OF SOME CREATURE

In Texas when I was twenty we went out
before dawn with the old ranchers,
parked on the shoulders of county roads
and choked bourbon and cold coffee.
At first light the wardens miles off
fired the signal shots; over our heads
the pennons of wings unfurled briskly
out of our dreams and into the mouths
the shotguns turned up to tatter them.

What are the rules? I cried in a rain
of pretty doves, the old men mirthful
with drink and powder, the dogs mad
running—and I learned there were none,
no limits until the time or the game
gave out. The black valley shuddered,
the doves were cadence and music,
the windshields lined up mile on mile
glittered like brass bells in a parade.

When guns stopped, everything stopped.
Bottles glowed neck-up in the ditches,
slopped coffee bled into the gravel,
the gentle birds like bits of high sky
murdered lay torn in the truck beds.
Armies of ranchers disbanded into dust
with shotguns broken; if you went back
any day after, you found shell cases
bleaching and white feathers light as air.

Today at dawn the call of some creature
perhaps a mourning dove, this evening

owls in the willow spying on darkness;
tomorrow—who knows what voice? Today,
at forty, I dreamed the dead ranchers
met in my sleep to hunt the whitewings
—passing a last bottle, ready forever
to rouse up the days of all our lives
going armed and aimless against the sun.

A LETTER FROM EXILE

Love, getting on, living abroad—
Everything in the end comes down
To one religion or another; gods
Move in and out of our gray rooms
Like old mistresses—regardless
Of how our tastes change, ritual
Sleeps beside us, rises with us,
Makes our breakfasts and shares
With us the view out the window
In whichever country of the mind
Fate chooses us. All things seen
Assume diverse neutralities;
Under them resides the same
Nationless order called divine.

THE ISLANDS

They fall and rise
against the bow's motion—
miles off, an emptiness
the wind feeds our sail.
Spending our idleness

we meet day after day
on the same boat-dock,
burdened with baskets,
sweater arms tied
around our sunburnt necks;

and up at the cottage
we have said our goodbyes
with kisses to mothers
and fathers. We crouch
in the dinghy, the oars

hauling us to the sloop;
ashore, the dog barks
and runs off his grief
at the edge of the sand,
too obedient to swim out.

Now it is the ocean
concerns us. The islands.
Inside an hour's sailing
we can make them out
between us and the sun—

solemn and irregular
they lie at the limits
of vision; they lull us
with their rocking.
We speculate on them.

We know, through glasses,
pines grow there, tall
but leaning landward;
sometimes we see white wings
disperse from the shade.

Shall we two settle there?
We talk, me at the tiller,
you with your gaze set
across the gray water.
O shall we live forever?

PITT POETRY SERIES
Ed Ochester, General Editor

Tom Lowenstein, tr., *Eskimo Poems from Canada and Greenland*
Archibald MacLeish, *The Great American Fourth of July Parade*
Peter Meinke, *Night Watch on the Chesapeake*
Peter Meinke, *Trying to Surprise God*
Judith Minty, *In the Presence of Mothers*
Carol Muske, *Camouflage*
Carol Muske, *Wyndmere*
Leonard Nathan, *Carrying On: New & Selected Poems*
Leonard Nathan, *Dear Blood*
Leonard Nathan, *Holding Patterns*
Kathleen Norris, *The Middle of the World*
Sharon Olds, *Satan Says*
Alicia Ostriker, *The Imaginary Lover*
Greg Pape, *Black Branches*
Greg Pape, *Border Crossings*
James Reiss, *Express*
William Pitt Root, *Faultdancing*
Liz Rosenberg, *The Fire Music*
Dennis Scott, *Uncle Time*
Herbert Scott, *Groceries*
Richard Shelton, *Of All the Dirty Words*
Richard Shelton, *Selected Poems, 1969-1981*
Richard Shelton, *You Can't Have Everything*
Arthur Smith, *Elegy on Independence Day*
Gary Soto, *Black Hair*
Gary Soto, *The Elements of San Joaquin*
Gary Soto, *The Tale of Sunlight*
Gary Soto, *Where Sparrows Work Hard*
Tomas Tranströmer, *Windows & Stones: Selected Poems*
Chase Twichell, *Northern Spy*
Chase Twichell, *The Odds*
Leslie Ullman, *Dreams by No One's Daughter*
Constance Urdang, *The Lone Woman and Others*
Constance Urdang, *Only the World*
Ronald Wallace, *People and Dog in the Sun*
Ronald Wallace, *Tunes for Bears to Dance To*
Cary Waterman, *The Salamander Migration and Other Poems*
Bruce Weigl, *A Romance*
Robley Wilson, Jr., *Kingdoms of the Ordinary*
David Wojahn, *Glassworks*
David P. Young, *The Names of a Hare in English*
Paul Zimmer, *Family Reunion: Selected and New Poems*